STEP·B

FRENCH
Cooking

Your Promise of Success

Welcome to the world of Confident Cooking, created for you
in our test kitchen, where recipes are double tested by our team of
home economists to achieve a high standard of success.

MURDOCH BOOKS
Sydney • London • Vancouver

BASIC FRENCH PANTRY

Most of the ingredients for French cooking are familiar to everyone and available everywhere. Anything that cannot be purchased at your local supermarket or delicatessen can usually be made at home or replaced with a suitable substitute.

Allspice: Berry which has the flavour of cloves, nutmeg and cinnamon. Used as a flavouring in sweet and savoury foods.

Bouquet Garni: Bunch of herbs used for flavouring dishes such as casseroles and sauces. Consists of parsley, thyme, bay leaf and peppercorns, tied in a muslin bag.

Chicken Pâté: Smooth chicken liver paste available from delicatessens and supermarket refrigerator sections.

Caramelise: To cook sugar slowly until it turns the colour of caramel.

Cracked Wheat: Whole wheat grains which have been cracked or broken open during the early stages of milling the flour. Used for its nutty texture. Also known as burghul.

Croustade: Fried bread or pastry case used to hold fillings.

Dill: Herb used to flavour soups, sauces, salads and pickles.

Eggplant: Egg-shaped vegetable with smooth shiny purple skin and creamy-white flesh. Also known as aubergine.

French Mustard: Condiment prepared from mustard seeds, herbs, oil and vinegar, used to flavour savoury dishes. French mustard is spicy but not 'hot'. The most famous French mustard comes from the town of Dijon and is always clearly labelled 'Dijon mustard'. It is milder than most mustards and perfect with delicate meats such as veal and chicken.

Gruyére Cheese: Hard cheese with a minimum fat content of 27 per cent. It is related to Emmenthal. Swiss Gruyére is sweeter than the French variety.

Gougére: Choux pastry made from water, fat and flour which forms a base for other ingredients.

Herbs: Unless otherwise specified use fresh herbs in these recipies. The predominant herbs in French cooking are those that make up a Bouquet Garni - parsley, thyme and bay leaves - as well as tarragon, dill and basil. If fresh herbs are not available, use 1/3 of the quantity specified of dried herbs, as they are stronger tasting.

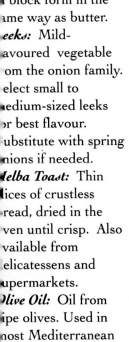

Pull: To remove the stem from the tops of strawberries.

Horseradish: Root of the horseradish plant. Commercially made horseradish is a mixture of grated horseradish root, oil, vinegar and sugar.

Lard: Commercial pig fat available from refrigerator sections of supermarkets. Sold in block form in the same way as butter.

Leeks: Mild-flavoured vegetable from the onion family. Select small to medium-sized leeks for best flavour. Substitute with spring onions if needed.

Melba Toast: Thin slices of crustless bread, dried in the oven until crisp. Also available from delicatessens and supermarkets.

Olive Oil: Oil from ripe olives. Used in most Mediterranean styles of cooking.

Parmesan Cheese: Hard cheese used to flavour foods. Available in block form or grated. Keeps well in block form. Strong in flavour. Use in moderation.

Watercress: Perennial green leafy plant of the mustard family which grows in streams. It has deep green rounded leaves and a peppery flavour. Use in sandwiches, salads or as a garnish.

Red Wine Vinegar: Refined vinegar made from red wine. Available from delicatessens and some supermarkets.

Tarragon: A flavourful herb, often used in chicken dishes. It is also used to flavour vinegar and is an important ingredient in Bearnaise sauce. When buying fresh tarragon, make sure it is French tarragon, not Russian. They look similar but Russian tarragon has very little flavour. French tarragon when crushed between the fingers will release a sweet pugent scent.

Vinaigrette: A salad dressing also called French dressing, which can be made in quantity in a food processor and stored in the refrigerator for several weeks. It is made from olive oil, wine vinegar, Dijon mustard and pepper. Proportions are usually 5 parts oil to 1 part vinegar. Olive oil hardens when it is refrigerated; soften 30 minutes before using.

3

Add onions to the pan and cook until well brown, approximately 20 minutes.

Add the garlic and sugar and stir through until the sugar has browned.

Add vinegar, flour, sherry, wine, consommé and water and stir until thick.

Brush oil over both sides of bread and sprinkle with the grated Parmesan.

SOUPS & SUPPERS

*These can be served as a first course or, with a salad,
a lunch or light supper dish.*

French Onion Soup

Preparation time:
15 minutes
Cooking time:
45 minutes
Serves 4-6

---

50 g butter
1 tablespoon olive oil
4 large brown onions,
thinly sliced
1 clove garlic, crushed
1 tablespoon sugar
2 tablespoons red
wine vinegar
1/3 cup plain flour
1/2 cup dry sherry
1 cup dry white wine
1 x 430 g can
beef consommé

1 1/4 cups water
2 tablespoons olive
oil, extra
1 clove garlic,
crushed, extra
1 small French bread
stick, cut into 2 cm
slices
1/2 cup grated
Parmesan cheese
parsley, to garnish

1 Heat butter and olive oil together in a large frypan. Add onions, cook about 20 minutes until brown. 2 Add garlic and sugar, stir through until sugar has browned. Add vinegar, cook 2 minutes. Sprinkle flour over the onions, cook stirring for 1 minute. Stir in the sherry, white wine, consommé and water. Continue stirring until mixture boils and thickens, reduce heat and simmer the soup uncovered for about 25 minutes. 3 Preheat oven to 210°C. Combine extra olive oil and garlic in a small bowl. Brush over both sides of bread, sprinkle one side with Parmesan. Bake 5 minutes or until crisp and golden. 4 To serve, place a slice of bread at the bottom of each soup bowl, pour over soup, garnish with parsley.

HINT
It is important that the onions are well browned to give the soup an authentic flavour. The sugar helps to caramelise the onions. Start with full heat for the initial cooking then reduce to medium heat to brown the onions slowly. The garlic bread with Parmesan can also be served as an accompaniment to many other dishes, especially salads. It's more nourishing and filling than normal garlic bread.

Prawn Croustade

Serve as an entrée.

Preparation time:
45 minutes
Cooking time:
25 minutes
Serves 6

---

*½ loaf unsliced
  bread
½ cup olive oil
1 clove garlic, crushed*

*FILLING
500 g green prawns
1 ½ cups water
2 slices lemon
50 g butter*

*6 spring onions
3 tablespoons plain
  flour
ground pepper
1 tablespoon lemon
  juice
1 teaspoon dried dill
¼ cup cream
parsley and lemon, to
  garnish*

---

1 Preheat oven to 210°C. Remove crust from bread, cut into 5 cm thick slices. Cut each slice diagonally to form a triangle. Cut a 1 cm border around the bread slices, scoop out centre, taking care to leave a base. This gives a cavity in which to place prawn filling. Heat oil and garlic together in a small pan, brush all over bread case. Bake 10 minutes.

2 To make Filling: Shell and devein prawns and chop roughly. Place in a small pan and cover with water. Add lemon slices, simmer 15 minutes, strain and reserve liquid.

3 Heat butter in a small pan, cook chopped spring onions until soft, add flour and pepper. Stir over low heat 2 minutes. Gradually add reserved prawn liquid. Stir constantly over medium heat 5 minutes or until sauce boils and thickens. Add lemon juice, dill, cream and prawns and heat gently for approximately 5 minutes.

4 To serve, spoon filling into bread cases, garnish with parsley and lemon.

Scoop out centre of bread triangles taking care to leave a base.

Chop spring onions and cook until soft in butter then add flour and pepper.

Add lemon juice, dill, cream and prawns
to the thickened sauce and heat 5 mins.

Spoon filling into the centre of the baked
bread cases just before serving.

Tomato and Olive Flan

A hearty robust dish.

Preparation time:
20 minutes + 30 minutes standing
Cooking time:
30-35 minutes
Makes 1 x 20 cm flan

PASTRY
2 cups plain flour
90 g butter, chopped
1 egg yolk
1 tablespoon water

FILLING
2 tablespoons olive oil
1 tablespoon French mustard
6 anchovy fillets, mashed

15 g butter
6 small tomatoes peeled and chopped
3 large onions, thinly sliced
1 teaspoon sugar
2 tablespoons shredded fresh basil
1 cup stoned olives, sliced
1 cup grated Gruyére cheese

---

1 Preheat oven to 210°C. Brush a 20 cm deep flan tin with melted butter or oil. Coat base and sides evenly with flour; shake off any excess. To make Pastry: Place flour and butter into food processor bowl; using pulse action, press button for 30 seconds or until mixture has a fine crumbly texture. Add the combined egg yolk and water, process 30 seconds or until mixture comes together. Briefly knead on a lightly floured surface. Store, covered with plastic wrap in refrigerator 30 minutes.

2 To make Filling: Combine oil, mustard and anchovy fillets into a smooth paste either with a fork in a bowl or in a food processor. Roll pastry out to fit 20 cm flan tin. Cover pastry with a large sheet of greaseproof paper. Spread a layer of dried beans evenly over paper. Bake 15 minutes. Remove from oven. Discard paper and beans. Cool. Spread mustard-anchovy mixture over base of pastry. Heat butter in a medium pan, cook tomatoes and onion until soft. Remove from heat. Drain off excess liquid. Spoon tomato mixture over pastry base. Mix together the sugar, basil and olives; sprinkle over the tomato mixture. Top with cheese.

3 Bake for 20 minutes or until pastry is crisp and cheese browned.

> ### HINT
> To peel tomatoes, mark a small cross on the top, place in a bowl, pour over boiling water and leave for 1-2 minutes. Immediately plunge into cold water. Remove and peel skin from top.

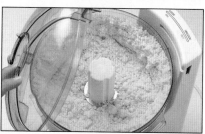

Process flour and butter until the mixture
has a fine crumbly texture.

With floured hands, knead the dough
briefly on a lightly floured surface.

Spread the mustard-anchovy mixture
over the base of the pastry.

Spoon the tomato and onions over the
anchovy mixture before adding olives.

Chilled Cod Pâté with Melba Toast

Ideal as an entrée.

Preparation time:
10 minutes +
chilling
Cooking time:
15 minutes
Serves 4-6

---

500 g smoked cod
1/4 cup olive oil
1 clove garlic, crushed
2 tablespoons plain
flour
1/4 cup lemon juice

1 cup milk
Melba Toast (see
HINT)
lemon and dill, to
serve

---

1 Cover fish with cold water in a large pan. Bring slowly to simmer, cook uncovered 10-15 minutes. Strain water, flake the flesh and remove bones.
2 Heat oil in a large pan, add garlic and flaked fish, stir 1 minute. Add flour and stir over a low heat. Add lemon juice gradually to the pan, stirring until the mixture is smooth. Add milk gradually and stir until mixture boils and thickens.
3 Pour mixture into food processor bowl and process 30 seconds until smooth.

Spoon into individual serving dishes (1/2 cup capacity) and refrigerate until firm. Serve with Melba Toast and garnish with lemon and dill.

HINT
Melba Toast can be bought at supermarkets. To make your own, remove the crusts from slices of fresh bread. Flatten with a rolling pin and cut into desired shapes. Dry bread in a 220°C oven for 10 minutes.
Alternatively toast white sandwich bread on both sides, remove crusts and slice through the centre with a serrated knife so that each slice is very thin and toasted on one side only. Toast the other side lightly.

Flake the flesh of the smoked cod with a fork and remove any bones.

Add flour to the fish and garlic in the pan and stir over low heat.

Gradually add the milk, stirring until the mixture boils and thickens.

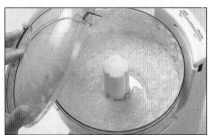

Pour mixture into food processor bowl and process 30 seconds until smooth.

Ham and Mushroom Gougére

Preparation time:
40 minutes
Cooking time:
30-40 minutes
Serves 4-6

PASTRY	3 tablespoons plain
75 g butter	*flour*
1 cup water	*1 cup chicken stock*
1 cup plain flour	*2 teaspoons French*
3 eggs, lightly beaten	*mustard*
	250 g ham, shredded
FILLING	*1 medium tomato*
30 g butter	*peeled, seeded and*
1 onion, chopped	*chopped*
250 g mushrooms,	*1 tablespoon chopped*
chopped	*fresh basil or thyme*

1 Preheat oven to 210°C. Brush a deep 25 cm square ovenproof dish with melted butter or oil. To make Pastry: Heat butter and water until boiling; remove from heat and add flour. Beat vigorously, making sure the flour is thoroughly incorporated. Cool slightly. Add eggs a little at a time, beating well after each addition. Spread thinly over the base and sides of the prepared dish.

2 To make Filling: Heat butter in a medium pan. Add onion, cook stirring for 1 minute; add mushrooms, cover and cook 3 minutes. Uncover, stir through flour. When blended, add chicken stock. Stir to form a smooth sauce, simmer 3 minutes. Add mustard, ham, tomato and basil.

3 Pour filling over pastry base. Bake 30 minutes, reduce temperature to 180°C and bake a further 10-15 minutes or until pastry puffs and browns. Serve as soon as you remove it from the oven.

Off the heat, beat flour vigorously and thoroughly into the butter and water.

Add the eggs, a little at a time, beating well after each addition.

Stir flour into onion and mushroom mixture and then add chicken stock.

Add mustard, ham, tomato and basil to the sauce and stir to combine.

13

Cheese Soufflés with Crab Sauce

Preparation time:
  35 minutes
Cooking time:
  15-20 minutes
Serves 6

---

3 tablespoons dried
  breadcrumbs
20 g butter
¼ cup plain flour
1 cup milk
3 tablespoons grated
  Parmesan cheese
90 g Cheddar cheese,
  grated
1 teaspoon French
  mustard
3 eggs, separated

CRAB SAUCE
130 g butter
2 tablespoons plain
  flour
1 teaspoon ground
  sweet paprika
¾ cup chicken stock
½ cup cream
2 tablespoons sherry
ground pepper, to
  taste
1 x 200 g can of crab
  meat, well drained

---

1 Preheat oven to 180°C. Prepare 6 (½ cup capacity) soufflé dishes with melted butter. Coat base and sides evenly with dried breadcrumbs. Shake off any excess.

2 Heat butter in a small pan; add flour. Stir over a low heat 2 minutes or until mixture is lightly golden. Add milk gradually, stirring until mixture is smooth. Stir constantly over medium heat until sauce boils and thickens; boil further 1 minute; remove from heat. Add cheeses and mustard. Beat through egg yolks. Transfer mixture to large bowl.

3 Place egg whites in a small, clean dry mixer bowl. Beat until soft peaks form. Using a metal spoon, gradually fold gently through the cheese mixture and pour immediately into the prepared soufflé dishes. Bake 10-15 minutes or until set and golden. Serve soufflés immediately with Crab Sauce as they quickly lose volume once they leave the oven.

4 To make Crab Sauce: Heat butter in a small pan; stir in flour and paprika. Stir through stock, cream and sherry and cook until mixture boils and thickens. Stir in drained crab, season with pepper and serve immediately.

Note: This soufflé can be cooked in a 14 cm soufflé dish for approximately 45 minutes instead. Soufflés should wobble slightly and the centre should be moist when cooked. Soufflés can be prepared up to Step 2 ahead of time. Gently heat base ingredients before adding beaten egg whites.

Coat base and sides of soufflé dishes with breadcrumbs and shake off excess.

Off the heat, add cheeses and mustard and beat through the egg yolks.

Place egg whites in a clean dry mixer bowl and beat until soft peaks form.

Using a metal spoon, gradually fold the egg whites through the egg mixture.

Potato Omelette with Olive Topping

Preparation time:
20 minutes
Cooking time:
20 minutes
Serves 4-6

---

2 tablespoons olive oil
3 rashers bacon,
　finely chopped
2 medium potatoes,
　diced
1 medium onion,
　thinly sliced
6 eggs, lightly beaten
2 tablespoons milk
ground pepper, to
　taste

OLIVE TOPPING
1/2 cup stoned olives
1 tablespoon capers
1 x 425 g can tuna in
　brine, drained
1/4 cup olive oil
1/4 cup lemon juice
1/2 cup chopped
　parsley
lemon slices, to
　garnish

---

1 Heat oil in a heavy-based deep omelette pan. Add bacon, cook until golden, remove. Add potatoes and cook, stirring often until golden, remove. Add onion and cook until brown. Return bacon and potatoes to the pan.

2 Whisk the eggs and milk together, pour over the bacon and potato mixture, season with pepper, cover pan with lid or foil, reduce heat to low and cook 10-15 minutes or until mixture has set.

3 To make Olive Topping: Place olives, capers, tuna, oil and lemon juice into food processor bowl. Process 30 seconds or until mixture is a smooth spreading consistency.

4 To serve, spread set omelette with topping, sprinkle with chopped parsley, garnish with lemon slices and cut into wedges to serve.

Note: The Olive Topping is called *Tapenade* in France and is often served with hard-boiled eggs as an appetiser. Try it also as a spread on crackers or toast.

Add potatoes to the pan and cook, stirring often, until golden.

Return the cooked bacon to the potatoes and onions in the pan.

Whisk the eggs and milk together, pour over the bacon and potato mixture.

Process olives, capers, tuna, oil and lemon juice until mixture is smooth.

17

Leek Tart

Serve piping hot.

Preparation time:
30 minutes
Cooking time:
30-40 minutes
Makes 1 x 23 cm flan

PASTRY
2 ½ cups plain flour
150 g butter, chopped
2 tablespoons lemon
  juice
1 tablespoon water

FILLING
30 g butter
2 rashers bacon,
  finely chopped
4 leeks, finely sliced

1 tablespoon white
  wine vinegar
¼ cup plain flour
1 cup milk
2 eggs, lightly beaten
1 cup grated Cheddar
  cheese
1 teaspoon ground
  black pepper
beaten egg, for glaze
herbs, to garnish

---

1 Preheat oven to 210°C. Brush a shallow 23 cm round fluted flan tin with melted butter or oil. To make Pastry: Place flour and butter into food processor bowl. Using the pulse action press button for 30 seconds or until mixture has a fine crumbly texture. Add lemon juice and almost all the water, process 30 seconds until mixture is smooth. Refrigerate, covered with plastic wrap for 30 minutes.

2 To make Filling: Heat butter in a medium pan, add bacon, cook until crisp. Add leeks, cook for 5 minutes or until leeks are soft. Stir through vinegar and flour. Remove from heat. Add milk gradually, stir until smooth. Return to heat, stir until sauce boils and thickens. Allow filling to cool slightly. Stir in eggs, cheese and pepper.

3 Roll ⅔ of pastry to line flan tin. Spoon filling over pastry base. Roll out remaining ⅓ pastry to cover top of pie. Trim and decorate edges, glaze with beaten egg. Cut three deep slits in pastry to allow steam to escape. Bake 30-40 minutes until crust is golden brown and crisp.

4 To serve, cut into wedges and garnish with fresh herbs.

HINT
Leeks have a mild onion flavour and when cooked slowly in butter, a creamy texture. The white part of the leek is the most tender, but you can use about 5 cm of the green. Above that the green part is too fibrous.
Leeks require thorough washing before using. Slit into the fleshy parts and shred almost to base. This loosens the layers so that soil can be easily removed when rinsed under a tap.

Process flour and butter for 30 seconds or until mixture has crumbly texture.

Roll out two-thirds of the pastry to line the flan tin.

Add leeks to the crispy bacon in the pan and cook for approximately 5 minutes.

Spoon the slightly cooled filling over the pastry base.

Place lemon slices, onion, garlic and thyme into gutted fish cavity.

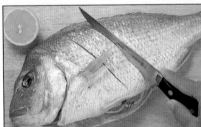

Score the thickest part of the fish with two diagonal slashes on both sides.

Stir in sugar, anchovies, wine, tomatoes and their juice, lemon juice and thyme.

Pour sauce over the prepared fish and bake for approximately 20 minutes.

SEAFOOD

French seafood dishes usually come with a sauce, either cooked with the fish or poured over. It helps to keep the seafood moist.

Baked Snapper with Garlic and Tomatoes

Preparation time:
25 minutes
Cooking time:
30-40 minutes
Serves 4-6

---

1 x 1 kg whole snapper
3 slices lemon
1 small onion, thickly sliced
1 clove garlic
1 sprig fresh thyme
1 tablespoon olive oil

SAUCE
2 tablespoons olive oil
1 clove garlic, crushed
1 small onion, chopped

1 teaspoon sugar
3 anchovies, mashed
1/2 cup white wine
1 x 440 g can tomatoes, chopped, juice reserved
4 tablespoons lemon juice
sprig fresh thyme
extra thyme leaves and lemon slices, to garnish

---

1 Preheat oven to 200°C. To prepare Fish: Remove any loose scales, trim tail to a V shape, remove fins. Wipe out gut area with damp absorbent paper. Place lemon slices, onion, garlic clove and thyme into gutted cavity. Score the thickest part of the fish with two diagonal slashes. Turn fish over and slash other side. Rub outside of fish with olive oil. Place in baking dish.

2 To make Sauce: Heat oil in pan, add garlic and onion and cook stirring until onion browns. Stir in sugar, anchovies, white wine, chopped tomatoes, reserved tomato juice, lemon juice and fresh thyme. Simmer uncovered until sauce is reduced by 1/3 and thickened slightly.

3 Pour Sauce over the prepared fish. Bake for 20 minutes or until fish flakes easily when loosened with a fork. Serve on a heated platter, garnish with thyme leaves and lemon slices.

HINT
This dish can be served either hot or cold. Many people don't think of serving fish cold, but it is delicious. It is important to serve it at room temperature, not chilled. Cook as above, cover and set aside until it cools .

Fish Fillets with Butter Sauce

Preparation time:
  30 minutes
Cooking time:
  30-40 minutes
Serves 4

---

*4 medium white fish
  fillets (about 150 g
  each)*
1/4 cup plain flour
*ground pepper, to
  taste*
60 g butter
1 cup Fish Stock
*4 tablespoons lemon
  juice*
2 egg yolks
1/4 cup cream
*1/2 cup chopped
  parsley*

*lemon and lime, for
  garnish*

FISH STOCK
*200 g fish trimmings
  (see Note)*
2 slices lemon
1 bay leaf
1 1/2 cups water
1/2 cup white wine
6 peppercorns
parsley stalks

---

1 Toss fillets lightly in flour which has been seasoned with pepper. Shake off any excess.
2 Heat butter in a large frypan. When butter is golden brown add the fish fillets, cook over a medium-high heat 1 minute each side; remove and drain on absorbent paper.
3 Add any remaining flour to the pan juices, stir through. Pour in the stock and lemon juice; stir until simmering. Stir combined egg yolks and cream through the sauce. Heat gently, add fish fillets to sauce and simmer uncovered until fish is cooked, about 5-10 minutes, depending on the thickness of the fillets. Serve on a heated plate, garnished with chopped parsley, lemon and lime. Accompany with extra sauce in a sauce boat.
4 To make Stock: Place fish trimmings, lemon slices, bay leaf, water, white wine, peppercorns and parsley stalks into a pan. Simmer uncovered for 20 minutes. Strain. Remeasure, add water if necessary to make up to 1 cup.
Note: Fish trimmings are literally trimmings from filleted fish and are available from your fish shop.

HINT
Before cooking the fillets, the butter must be golden brown – this gives a characteristic 'nutty' taste to the fish. Fish stock should only be cooked for 20 minutes. Unlike beef or chicken stock, which require long cooking, to extract the flavour, fish stock is quick to make. Make sure your trimmings are from white, non-oily fish.

When the butter is golden, add the fish fillets and cook for 1 minute each side.

Add remaining flour to the pan juices and stir through thoroughly.

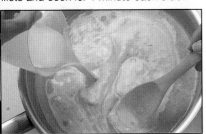

Stir the combined egg yolks and cream through the sauce and heat gently.

Garnish the fish with thin slices of lemon and lime.

Trout with Almonds

Preparation time:
15 minutes
Cooking time:
15 minutes
Serves 4

---

4 trout
approximately
200 g each, gutted
and scaled
1/4 cup plain flour
ground pepper, to
taste
1/2 teaspoon dried
dill leaves
1/4 teaspoon mustard
powder

5 tablespoons lemon
juice
90 g butter
1/2 cup blanched
halved almonds
1/2 cup dry white
wine
lemon slices, to
garnish
dill or parsley sprigs,
to garnish

---

1 Using scissors remove the fins from the trout, trim the tail, wipe over the surface of the fish with damp absorbent paper to remove any loose scales. Season flour with pepper, dill and mustard powder.

2 Brush surface of fish with lemon juice and reserve any excess. Coat whole trout in seasoned flour to form a crust. Shake to discard any excess flour.

3 Heat butter in a large pan, add almonds and cook stirring until golden. Remove from heat. Drain almonds on absorbent paper. Add fish to pan, cook over medium-high heat until tender, turning once, and being careful not to break them. Remove from pan and drain well on absorbent paper.

4 Add remaining lemon juice and the wine to pan, simmer uncovered over a high heat until reduced by half, add reserved almonds and pour over fish immediately. Serve at once garnished with lemon slices and dill or parsley sprigs.

Using scissors, remove the fins and trim the tail from the trout.

Coat trout in flour seasoned with dill, pepper and mustard to form a crust.

Cook fish over medium-high heat until tender, turning once.

Simmer lemon juice and wine uncovered over high heat until reduced by half.

Tie the meat with string to help hold its shape while cooking.

Add meat to oil in pan and quickly brown all over to seal in juices.

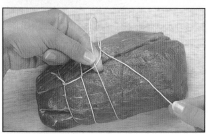

Spread the top surface of the cooled meat with pâté.

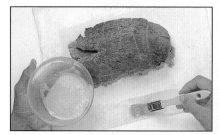

Place meat, pâté-side down onto the pastry, glaze edges with egg and seal.

MEAT & POULTRY

*The French make the most of meat and poultry, using not only the expensive cuts,
but the cheaper ones too, in cassoulets and stews.*

Beef Fillet in a Pastry Crust with Horseradish Cream

Preparation time:
20 minutes
Cooking time:
30-45 minutes
Serves 6

750 g whole piece beef fillet	SAUCE
1 clove garlic, crushed	1 cup light sour cream
3 tablespoons olive oil	1 tablespoon bottled or grated horseradish (see Note)
1 teaspoon ground pepper	
100 g chicken pâté	
1 x 375 g packet puff pastry	1 tablespoon chopped chives
beaten egg for glazing	

1 Preheat oven to 210°C. Trim meat of excess fat. Tie meat with string to help hold its shape while cooking. Rub the surface of meat with garlic, 1 tablespoon oil and pepper.

2 Heat remaining oil in a large pan. Add meat and quickly brown all over on high heat to seal in juices, about 5 minutes. Set aside to cool. Remove string.

3 Roll pastry into a rectangle about 40 x 30 cm or large enough to encase the meat. Spread the top surface of the cooled meat with pâté. Place meat pâté-side-down onto pastry, glaze edges with egg and seal. Place on a baking tray pâté-side-up, glaze and decorate with pastry off-cuts. Bake 25-35 minutes. Stand 10 minutes before carving into 2 cm thick slices and serve with accompanying Sauce.

4 To make Sauce: Mix together the sour cream, horseradish and chives and beat well to combine. Transfer to sauceboat or pretty bowl.

Note: If horseradish is unavailable, add 2 tablespoons of French mustard to the cream as a substitute.

> ### HINT
> Use eye fillet rather than Scotch fillet for this dish because it is leaner. The butter in the chicken pâté and puff pastry will keep the meat moist.

Beef and Red Wine Casserole

Preparation time:
25 minutes
Cooking time:
1½ hours
Serves 6

---

*1 kg blade steak
2 rashers bacon
2 tablespoons olive oil
12 small pickling
  onions, peeled
2 cloves garlic,
  crushed
1/3 cup plain flour
2 cups red wine*

*1 teaspoon fresh
  thyme leaves
1 tablespoon grated
  or bottled
  horseradish
30 g butter
375 g button
  mushrooms
fresh thyme, to
  garnish*

---

1 Trim meat of excess fat and cut into 1.5 cm cubes. Cut bacon into 1 cm strips.

2 Heat oil in a large pan, add bacon, cook until brown; remove. Add onions to pan and cook in bacon fat until well browned; remove. Add garlic and cook 1 minute. Cook meat pieces in remaining fat to colour; stir through flour. Stir in red wine, thyme and horseradish, stir until mixture boils and thickens. Return onions and bacon to pan, reduce heat, cover and simmer for 1 hour.

3 Heat butter in a small pan, add mushrooms and cook until soft. Stir mushrooms and juices through casserole, cook uncovered a further 30 minutes.

4 Serve casserole garnished with fresh thyme and accompany with fresh vegetables.

HINT
Rabbit or hare can be used in place of beef steak. Casseroles benefit from standing overnight when cooking time is completed as this encourages the flavour to fully develop.

Cut beef into 1.5 cm cubes and bacon into 1 cm strips.

Heat oil in a large pan, add bacon and cook until brown.

Add red wine, thyme and horseradish and stir until mixture boils and thickens.

Thirty minutes before serving, add mushrooms cooked in butter.

Pepper Steak

Quickly made.

Preparation time:
15 minutes
Cooking time:
15 minutes
Serves 6

6 fillet, rump or sirloin steaks	1/4 cup dry sherry or brandy
50 g butter	1 cup beef stock
1 clove garlic, crushed	2 tablespoons green peppercorns
1 onion, chopped	1/2 cup cream
3 tablespoons plain flour	parsley, to garnish

1 Trim meat of excess fat. Heat butter in a large heavy frypan. Add garlic and onion, cook 1 minute. Add steaks and cook over high heat 2 minutes on each side; remove from pan. Remove pan from heat and stir flour through pan juices. Return pan to heat and cook until flour browns.

2 Pour in brandy and stock, stir until mixture comes to the boil; reduce heat and simmer 5 minutes. Add peppercorns and cream and stir, crushing peppercorns lightly with a spoon.

3 Return steaks to sauce and cook about 7-12 minutes.

Add steaks to garlic and onion and cook over high heat for 2 minutes each side.

Stir flour through pan juices, return pan to heat and cook until flour browns.

Add peppercorns and cream and stir,
crushing peppercorns lightly.

Return steaks to the sauce and cook for
7-12 minutes or as desired.

Cassoulet

Make and freeze.

Preparation time:
25 minutes
Cooking time:
2 hours
Serves 6

---

300 g chicken thigh fillets
300 g lean lamb
300 g lean pork loin
60 g lard
2 medium onions, chopped
2 cloves garlic, crushed
2 sticks celery, chopped
1 tablespoon plain flour
1 x 440 g can tomatoes, drained, juice reserved

1 cup white wine
1 teaspoon fresh thyme leaves
2 bay leaves
3 cloves
ground pepper, to taste
1 x 410 g can white cannellini beans, drained
200 g chopped pickled pork
100 g salami, chopped

---

1 Trim meat of excess fat and cut into 2 cm cubes. Heat lard in large pan, cook chicken until brown; remove. Cook lamb until brown, remove. Cook pork until brown; remove.

2 Add onions to remaining fat in pan, cook until well browned. Add garlic and celery, stir 1 minute, remove. Sprinkle flour over base of pan. Add chopped tomatoes, tomato juice and wine; stir until sauce boils and thickens. Add thyme, bay leaves, cloves and pepper. Bring to boil, reduce heat and simmer uncovered for 10 minutes.

3 Add meat, onion mixture and cannellini beans, cover and simmer 1 hour.

4 Remove lid, add pickled pork and salami; cover and cook for 30 minutes.

Trim chicken, lamb and pork of excess fat and cut into 2 cm cubes.

Add lamb to pan and cook, stirring, until it is brown, then remove.

Add thyme, bay leaves, cloves and pepper to the thickened sauce.

Add meat pieces, onion mixture and cannellini beans to the sauce.

33

Pork with Cabbage and Plums

Preparation time:
30 minutes
Cooking time:
1 ½ hours
Serves 4-6

1.5 kg pork loin
30 g butter
1 teaspoon allspice
½ cup water
30 g lard
1 large onion, thinly
sliced
500 g cabbage,
shredded
4 tablespoons lemon
juice

SAUCE
1 x 825 g can plums
in light syrup
30 g butter
4 spring onions,
finely chopped
¼ cup red wine
vinegar
1 chicken stock cube,
crumbled
¼ cup plain flour
¾ cup chicken stock

---

1 Preheat oven to 210°C. Remove visible fat and sinew from pork. Tie pork securely with string. Beat butter and allspice together, spread over pork surface, place meat onto a rack in a deep roasting pan. Add water to roasting pan. Bake 1¼ - 1½ hours or until juices run clear when meat is pierced with a skewer. Allow to stand 10 minutes.

2 Heat lard in a large pan, add onion and cook until brown. Add shredded cabbage and stir; add lemon juice. Cover, reduce heat and cook 10-15 minutes or until cabbage softens and becomes tender. Set aside and keep warm.

3 To make Sauce: Drain plums reserving the syrup, place plums in a heatproof casserole dish and set aside. Heat butter in a pan, add spring onions, cover and cook 1 minute on medium heat; add wine vinegar and cook 1 minute. Pour plum syrup and crumbled stock cube into pan, simmer uncovered 5 minutes. Place dish of plums in the oven for 15 minutes before serving to heat.

3 Carve meat into 3 mm slices reserving juices for gravy. Keep warm. Sprinkle flour over pan juices and cook until flour turns golden brown. Stir through chicken stock and plum sauce; bring to boil and simmer uncovered 5 minutes.

4 To serve, arrange cabbage over serving plate and overlap pork slices down the centre. Arrange whole plums around border and pour small amount of gravy over the pork. Serve the remaining sauce in a gravy boat.

Beat the butter and allspice together until it is smooth.

Spread the butter-allspice mixture over the securely tied pork.

Add shredded cabbage to the browned onion in the pan.

Pour reserved plum syrup and crumbled stock cube into the pan.

Veal with Dijon Mustard Sauce

Preparation time:
15 minutes
Cooking time:
20 minutes
Serves 6

---

6 veal steaks, 1 cm
thick
2 tablespoons plain
flour
ground pepper, to
taste
30 g butter
1 rasher bacon,
chopped
1 large onion,
chopped

1 cup white wine
1/2 cup chicken stock
1 teaspoon fresh
thyme leaves
3 tablespoons Dijon
mustard (see Note)
1/2 cup light or
reduced-fat cream
parsley, to garnish

---

1 Trim meat of excess fat. Toss meat in flour seasoned with pepper. Heat butter in pan; add bacon and onion, cook until golden brown. Remove. Add meat, cook on both sides until brown. Remove.

2 Sprinkle through any remaining seasoned flour, add wine and chicken stock, stir until mixture boils and thickens. Return bacon and onion to pan, add thyme leaves, mustard and cream. Return steaks to sauce and simmer gently until meat is tender, about 7-10 minutes.

3 Serve with vegetables in season and garnish with parsley.

Note: Dijon mustard is a mild aromatic mustard from the French town of Dijon. It is available in supermarkets. It is important to use it in this recipe because of its mild flavour. Veal is such a delicate meat that more robust mustards would overpower it.

If fresh thyme is not available, use a pinch of dried thyme.

Heat butter in pan, add bacon and onion and cook until golden brown.

Add the meat and cook on both sides until brown, then remove from pan.

Add thyme, mustard and cream to the sauce and stir through.

Return steaks to the sauce and simmer gently until the meat is tender.

Lamb Navarin (Lamb Casserole with Vegetables)

Preparation time:
20 minutes
Cooking time:
1 hour 45 minutes
Serves 6

1 kg lamb leg chops
30 g butter
1/4 cup olive oil
2 medium onions,
  chopped
1 clove garlic, crushed
2 parsnips, chopped
2 carrots, chopped
2 sticks celery,
  chopped
1/4 cup plain flour
1 x 440 g can
  tomatoes, drained,
  juice reserved
1/2 cup water

1 cup chicken stock
2 tablespoons chopped
  mint
1/2 cup frozen beans
1/2 cup chopped
  parsley
1 teaspoon fresh
  thyme leaves
ground pepper, to
  taste
1 tablespoon French
  mustard
1/2 cup chopped
  parsley, extra

1 Preheat oven to 150°C. Trim meat of excess fat and bones, cut into 2 cm cubes. Heat butter and oil in a large pan. Cook meat in batches over medium heat until well browned; drain on absorbent paper.

2 Cook onions until golden brown, add garlic, parsnips, carrots and celery; cook until all vegetables are lightly browned. Stir through flour, add roughly chopped tomatoes and reserved tomato juice, water, stock, mint, beans, parsley, thyme, pepper and mustard, to taste. Stir until sauce thickens.

3 Add meat, place in casserole dish, cover. Cook 1½ hours.

4 Serve with noodles and garnish with chopped parsley.

Note: This sauce may appear too thick, but as juices from meat are released, it will thin out.

Trim meat of excess fat and bones and cut into 2 cm cubes.

Cook meat in batches until well browned and drain on absorbent paper.

Add garlic, parsnips, carrots and celery and cook until lightly browned.

Add the browned meat to the sauce and cook in the oven for 1½ hours.

Roast Chicken with Grapes

A late summer dish.

Preparation time:
25 minutes + 15
minutes standing
Cooking time:
1½ hours
Serves 4-6

---

1 x 1.6 kg chicken
1 cup cracked wheat
1 cup boiling water
½ cup chopped chives
½ cup chopped parsley
2 teaspoons grated lemon rind
2 tablespoons lemon juice
1 teaspoon dried tarragon leaves
100 g seedless white grapes, halved
50 g butter, melted
ground pepper, to taste
1 egg, lightly beaten
2 teaspoons ground sweet paprika

SAUCE
¼ cup plain flour
½ cup dry white wine or dry cider
1 cup chicken stock
300 g seedless white grapes, halved
ground pepper, to taste
½ cup cream

---

1 Preheat oven to 180°C. Cover cracked wheat with boiling water and allow to stand 15 minutes. Drain off any excess water. Add chives, parsley, lemon rind, lemon juice, tarragon, grapes, all but 1 tablespoon of butter, pepper and egg. Mix together well.

2 Rinse chicken and remove any loose tissue from cavity. Spoon stuffing into cleaned cavity and tie wings and drumsticks securely into place with string. Brush with remaining butter, sprinkle with paprika. Place on roasting rack over baking dish and bake for 1¼-1½ hours or until cooked. Remove from pan and stand covered for 10 minutes before carving.

3 To make Sauce: Drain all but 3 tablespoons of fat from the pan. Sprinkle over flour, stir to smooth paste, cook stirring until flour turns golden brown. Add wine and stock, stir until sauce comes to the boil. Add grapes and pepper, simmer uncovered for 15 minutes. Add cream just before serving.

4 To serve, carve chicken and arrange on a warm serving plate with stuffing. Pour Sauce over chicken pieces and serve with roast vegetables.

HINT
Roast chicken and meats should stand for approximately 10 minutes before carving to prevent juice loss. Cover with foil.

Add beaten egg to the other stuffing
ingredients and mix well.

Spoon the grape stuffing into the cleaned
chicken cavity.

Add wine and stock to the sauce and stir
until the sauce comes to the boil.

Add halved grapes and ground pepper
to the sauce and simmer for 15 minutes.

Tarragon Cream Chicken

Preparation time:
  15 minutes
Cooking time:
  15-20 minutes
Serves 4

---

4 chicken breast fillets	*1 cup dry white wine*
1/3 cup plain flour	*1 cup chicken stock*
ground pepper, to taste	*1 1/2 teaspoons dried tarragon leaves*
60 g butter	*1/4 cup cream*
2 leeks, chopped	*fresh tarragon sprigs, to garnish*

1 Trim chicken fillets, toss in flour seasoned with pepper. Heat butter in a large pan until coloured. Add chicken fillets, cook over medium heat 3 minutes, turning once. Remove. Add leeks to pan and cook until slightly coloured, sprinkle through any remaining flour.

2 Pour wine and stock into pan, stir until mixture begins to simmer; add tarragon, simmer uncovered for 10 minutes.

3 Return chicken fillets to the pan, simmer uncovered 10-15 minutes or until tender. Add cream and garnish with tarragon sprigs.

Toss chicken fillets in flour which has been seasoned with pepper.

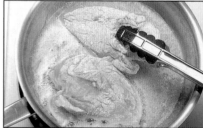

Cook chicken in butter over medium heat until golden on both sides.

Add remaining flour to leeks which have been cooked until slightly coloured.

Add tarragon to wine, stock and leek mixture and simmer for 10 minutes.

43

Chicken with Capsicum

Preparation time:
25 minutes
Cooking time:
40 minutes
Serves 6

---

1 kg chicken thigh fillets
1/4 cup oil
3 rashers bacon, finely chopped
2 large onions, thinly sliced
2 cloves garlic, crushed
2 small green capsicum, thinly sliced

2 small red capsicum, thinly sliced
1/4 cup plain flour
6 small ripe tomatoes, seeded and chopped
1 tablespoon sugar
2 tablespoons red wine vinegar
1 cup chicken stock
boiled rice, to serve
parsley, to garnish

---

1 Trim chicken of excess fat, cut into halves. Heat oil, add bacon and cook until crisp, remove. Add chicken to pan, cook until golden, remove. Add onions and garlic and cook until golden brown. Add capsicum strips, cover and cook 5 minutes.

2 Sprinkle flour over cooked capsicum and stir through, return bacon to the pan. Add tomatoes, sugar, wine vinegar and chicken stock. Bring to boil, reduce heat and simmer uncovered for 10 minutes. Transfer mixture to large pan.

3 Stir chicken pieces through sauce, continue to simmer uncovered for further 20 minutes or until chicken is tender.

4 Serve with boiled rice, garnish with parsley sprigs.

Note: Tomatoes don't have to be peeled for this dish but they should be seeded. Cut tomato in half and gently squeeze out the seeds. Any that remain can be easily removed with a teaspoon. This dish can be made ahead.

Trim chicken thigh fillets of excess fat and cut into halves.

Brown onion and garlic and add red and green capsicum strips.

Add tomatoes, sugar, vinegar and stock to the vegetables in the pan.

Stir chicken pieces through sauce and simmer for 20 minutes.

Break watercress into small sprigs,
Discarding the coarser stems.

Peel the cucumbers; halve them
lengthways and remove the seeds.

VEGETABLES

Often the French serve vegetables and salads as a course on their own. All of these dishes can be served on their own, as a first course or a light meal.

Watercress Salad

A tart-tasting salad.

Preparation time:
35 minutes
Chilling time:
30 minutes
Serves 4-6

1 bunch watercress	*DRESSING*
3 sticks celery	*1/4 cup olive oil*
1 cucumber	*1/4 cup lemon juice*
3 medium oranges	*2 teaspoons grated*
1 Spanish onion,	*orange rind*
thinly sliced and	*1 teaspoon seeded*
pushed into rings	*mustard*
3/4 cup chopped fresh	*ground pepper, to*
chives	*taste*
1/2 cup chopped	*1 tablespoon honey*
pecans or walnuts	

1 To make Salad: Wash and drain all vegetables. Break watercress into small sprigs, discard the coarser stems. Cut the celery into thin 5 cm long slices. Peel, halve and seed the cucumber and cut into 5 mm slices. Peel oranges, remove white membrane, and divide into segments. Place in refrigerator until needed.

2 To make Dressing: Combine oil, lemon juice, orange rind, mustard, pepper and honey in a screw top jar. Shake vigorously until well combined. Chill until needed.

3 Combine all salad ingredients in a serving bowl. Pour over dressing and toss. Sprinkle with pecans or walnuts.

Peel the oranges, taking care to remove all the white pith.

Separate orange segments by cutting between membrane and flesh.

Beans with Tomatoes

Preparation time:
10 minutes
Cooking time:
15 minutes
Serves 6

500 g green beans	*2 tablespoons red*
1 x 440 g can	*wine vinegar*
tomatoes	*1 tablespoon chopped*
2 tablespoons olive oil	*fresh basil*
1 large onion,	*1/4 cup chopped olives*
chopped	*ground pepper, to*
1 clove garlic, crushed	*taste*
2 teaspoons sugar	*basil sprigs, to garnish*

1 Trim tops and tails from beans and cut into halves. Cook in boiling water for 5 minutes, drain and rinse in cold water to refresh colour. Set aside. Chop tomatoes, reserving juice.

2 Heat oil in a pan, add onion and garlic, cook stirring until onion starts to brown. Sprinkle over sugar and cook until it caramelises. Add vinegar, cook 1 minute. Add tomatoes and juice, basil, olives and pepper. Simmer uncovered 5 minutes.

3 Add beans, simmer 10 minutes. Serve garnished with basil.

Trim tops and tails from beans and cut into halves.

Drain the tomatoes, reserving their juice and chop them.

Add tomatoes, basil, olives and pepper to the cooked onion.

Add the partially cooked beans to the sauce and simmer for 10 minutes.

Potato Cake

Serve with salad.

Preparation time:
20 minutes
Cooking time:
1 hour
Serves 4-6

---

8 medium potatoes
30 g butter
2 tablespoons olive
* oil*
1 clove garlic, crushed
1/2 teaspoon ground
* pepper*

2 cups dried
* breadcrumbs*
1 cup grated Cheddar
* cheese*
1/2 cup grated
* Parmesan cheese*

---

1 Preheat oven to 180°C. Brush a deep 20 cm springform tin with melted butter .

Line base and sides with greased paper. Peel potatoes and slice thinly.

2 In a small pan heat butter, oil, garlic and pepper. Overlap slices of potato over the base of tin. Brush with butter mixture. Sprinkle with mixed breadcrumbs and cheese. Continue layering potatoes, butter mixture and cheese mix, ending with the cheese mixture. Press down firmly with hand.
3 Bake for 1 hour or until golden on top. Serve warm.

Peel potatoes and slice thinly with a sharp knife.

Arrange potato in overlapping slices over base of tin.

Sprinkle each layer with combined cheeses and breadcrumbs.

Using your hand press the top layer of cheese mixture down firmly.

Ratatouille (Eggplant & Tomato Casserole)

Preparation time:
30 minutes + 30 minutes standing
Cooking time:
45 minutes
Serves 4-6

2 large eggplant (500g)
salt
2 medium zucchini, cut into 5 mm slices
½ cup olive oil
1 large brown onion, chopped
2 cloves garlic, crushed

2 teaspoons sugar
ground pepper, to taste
2 tablespoons red wine vinegar
2 medium ripe tomatoes, peeled, seeded and chopped
¼ cup white wine
¼ cup grated Parmesan cheese

1 Wash eggplant and cut into 1 cm slices, sprinkle with salt and allow to stand. Lightly salt sliced zucchini and stand 30 minutes. Wash salt from eggplant and zucchini, pat dry with absorbent paper.
2 Heat oil in frypan. Add onion and cook until golden brown. Add garlic and eggplant pieces and cook until brown, remove; cook zucchini slices until golden.
3 Transfer all vegetables to large pan. Sprinkle with sugar, pepper and vinegar. Add the tomatoes and wine. Cover and simmer for about 30 minutes.
4 Serve sprinkled with Parmesan.

HINT
This casserole may be served hot or cold. It can be served alone with French bread or as an accompaniment to meat or poultry dishes. Eggplant and zucchini can both taste bitter, depending upon their age. Salting them and leaving them to stand for about 30 minutes draws out their bitter juices. Rinse well.

Cut eggplant into 1 cm thick slices and sprinkle with salt.

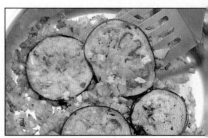

Add garlic and eggplant to onion in pan and cook until brown, then remove.

Add sugar, pepper and vinegar to the vegetables in the pan.

Add tomatoes and wine and simmer, covered, for 30 minutes.

Potato Puffs

Light and fluffy.

Preparation time:
    30 minutes
Cooking time:
    15 minutes
Serves 6

---

3 medium potatoes, peeled	*1 cup grated Gruyére cheese*
¾ cup water	*2 spring onions, chopped*
50 g butter	*½ teaspoon nutmeg*
¾ cup plain flour	*vegetable oil*
2 eggs, lightly beaten	

---

1 Cook potatoes in boiling water until tender, drain, mash and set aside.

2 Place water and butter into a pan, bring to the boil, add flour and stir over low heat. Allow mixture to cool slightly. Beat in eggs a little at a time. Transfer mixture to medium bowl.

3 Combine potato and egg mixtures, add cheese, spring onions and nutmeg.

4 Heat oil in a deep pan. Gently lower heaped tablespoons of mixture into hot oil and cook over medium high heat 5 minutes or until puffed and golden. Drain on absorbent paper. Serve immediately.

Add flour, all at once, to the butter and water mixture and stir well.

Allow mixture to cool slightly then beat in eggs a little at a time.

Add cheese, spring onions and nutmeg to the potato and egg mixture.

Deep fry tablespoons of the mixture until puffed and golden.

Remove core from peeled and quartered apples and brush with lemon juice.

Add milk or cream to the flour-egg mixture and blend in well.

Arrange apple quarters over pastry, sprinkle with icing sugar.

Pour egg mixture over partially baked apples and bake a further hour.

DESSERTS

Fresh fruit is best served at the end of a really rich meal. But for those special occasions, here are four spectacular French desserts.

French Apple Flan

Preparation time:
45 minutes
Cooking time:
1½ hours
Makes 1 x 23 cm flan

ALMOND PASTRY
1 ½ cups plain flour
1 cup ground almonds
2 tablespoons caster sugar
125 g unsalted butter, softened
1 tablespoon water

FILLING
5 medium green apples (see Note)

2 tablespoons lemon juice
2 tablespoons plain flour
4 eggs, lightly beaten
1 ¼ cups milk or cream
1 teaspoon imitation vanilla essence
½ cup pure icing sugar
½ teaspoon ground cinnamon

Preheat oven to 210°C. Brush a 23 cm deep flan tin with melted butter or oil. Coat base and sides evenly with flour; shake off any excess. To make Pastry: Place flour, almonds, sugar and butter into food processor bowl. Using the pulse action, press button for 30 seconds or until mixture has a fine crumbly texture. Add almost all the water, process 30 seconds until mixture is smooth. Store, covered with plastic wrap in refrigerator 30 minutes.

2 To make Filling: Peel and quarter apples, remove core and brush with lemon juice to prevent apples browning. In a medium mixing bowl, whisk flour and eggs together, add milk and essence, mix well.

3 Roll pastry between two sheets of plastic wrap. Press into prepared tin, lining base and sides. Arrange apple quarters over base. Sprinkle with icing sugar and cinnamon. Bake 30 minutes. Remove from oven, pour over egg mixture, reduce heat to 150°C and bake a further hour or until egg mixture is set.
Note: Substitute tinned apples, if preferred. If so, precook base for 10 minutes and cool before adding the apples and custard. Bake for 1 hour.

Crêpes Suzette

Preparation time:
  30 minutes
Cooking time:
  35 minutes
Serves 4-6

CREPE BATTER
1 cup plain flour
2 teaspoons caster
  sugar
2 eggs, lightly beaten
1 cup milk
15 g butter, melted
1 tablespoon brandy

SUZETTE SAUCE
60 g butter

1/4 cup sugar
1 tablespoon grated
  orange rind
1 tablespoon grated
  lemon rind
1 cup orange juice
1/4 cup lemon juice
1/2 cup Grand
  Marnier
cream and ice-cream,
  to serve

---

1 To make Batter: Place all ingredients into bowl of food processor. Using the pulse action, press button for 40 seconds or until ingredients are combined and the mixture is free of lumps. Transfer mixture to bowl or jug. Stand covered with plastic wrap for 1 hour. The crêpe batter should be the consistency of pouring cream. If batter thickens on standing, thin with milk or water.

2 To cook Crêpes: Pour 2-3 tablespoons batter onto lightly greased 10 cm crêpe pan; swirl evenly over the base. Cook over medium heat 1 minute or until underside is golden. Turn crêpe over, cook other side. Transfer to plate; cover with tea-towel, keep warm. Repeat process with remaining batter, greasing pan when necessary.

3 To make Sauce:

Heat butter in a pan, add sugar and stir over a medium heat until caramelised. Add the rinds, juices and Grand Marnier; simmer uncovered 10 minutes.

4 To Assemble: Preheat oven to 210°C. Fold crêpes into quarters and arrange across base of ovenproof dish, overlapping to form a pattern. Pour over Sauce. Bake 10-15 minutes and serve warm with cream or ice-cream.

HINT

Crêpes can be flambéd at the table, but be extremely careful. Heat 2 tablespoons of Grand Marnier, brandy or orange liqueur in a small pan or Turkish coffee warmer, light at the table and pour over the crêpes.

This crêpe batter can be used for all sweet crêpe recipes. Serve with the filling of your choice accompanied by cream or ice-cream.

To make the batter, place all ingredients into bowl of food processor.

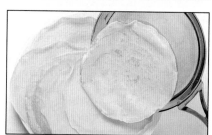

Cook crêpes until golden on both sides. Transfer to plate and cover.

Add orange and lemon juice to the caramelised butter-sugar mixture.

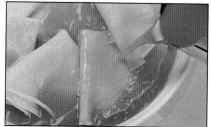

Fold crêpes into quarters, arrange them on ovenproof dish and pour over sauce.

Chilled Grand Marnier Soufflé

A spectacular dessert.

Preparation time:
35 minutes + 2-4
hour setting
Cooking time:
10 minutes
Serves 6

---

4 eggs, separated
1/4 cup caster sugar
1 teaspoon imitation
vanilla essence
1/2 cup Grand
Marnier
1 tablespoon grated
orange rind
1 cup orange juice
1 tablespoon gelatine
1/4 cup water

1 1/4 cups cream,
whipped
whipped cream,
extra
toasted flaked
almonds
glacé orange slices, to
decorate
brandy snaps to
accompany soufflés

---

1 Cut a piece of aluminium foil 5 cm longer than the circumference of a deep 18 cm (6 cup capacity) soufflé dish. Fold foil in half lengthways. Wrap foil around the outside of soufflé dish; it should extend 5 cm above the rim. Secure with string. Lightly grease the base and side of soufflé dish and foil with vegetable oil.

2 Beat egg yolks, sugar, essence, Grand Marnier, orange rind and juice together in a glass bowl over barely simmering water until mixture thickens. Sprinkle gelatine over water in a small bowl. Stand in hot water; stir until dissolved. Add to egg mixture. Chill mixture over ice, stirring occasionally until mixture begins to set.

3 Place egg whites in small dry mixer bowl. Beat until stiff peaks form. Fold in cream and gelatine mixture. Spoon into prepared soufflé dish. Refrigerate several hours or overnight until firm.

4 To serve, carefully remove collar from dish, decorate top of soufflé with extra whipped cream, toasted flaked almonds and glacé orange slices. Serve with brandy snaps or other sweet biscuits. **Note:** The foil collar holds the soufflé in place above the dish until it has set. Remove it carefully.

HINT

Working with gelatine is not difficult if you follow a few simple rules. First sprinkle the gelatine over cold water. This will soften it and prevent lumps from forming. Then stand the bowl of softened gelatine in hot water and stir until it has dissolved.
Grand Marnier is a French liqueur with an orange flavour.

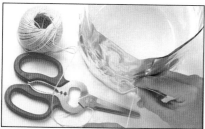

Wrap foil around outside of soufflé dish and secure with string.

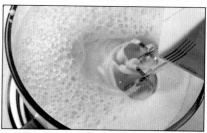

Beat egg yolk mixture over barely simmering water until thick.

Sprinkle the gelatine over cold water in a small bowl to soften.

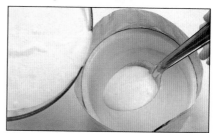

Spoon the mixture into the prepared soufflé dish and refrigerate.

Fritters with Strawberry Sauce

Preparation time:
30 minutes
Cooking time:
35 minutes
Serves 6-8

FRITTERS
1 cup water
60 g butter
1/4 cup caster sugar
1/2 cup currants
1 teaspoon grated orange rind
1 cup plain flour
3 eggs, lightly beaten

SAUCE
1/4 cup caster sugar

1/4 cup water
1 x 250 g punnet strawberries
2 tablespoons brandy or strawberry liqueur
oil, to deep-fry
icing sugar, to dust
whipped cream, to serve

1 To make Fritters: Place water, butter, sugar, currants and grated orange rind in a small pan; bring to boil. Stir in flour and beat until smooth using a wooden spoon. Cool slightly, gradually add the eggs, beating well after each addition; set aside.

2 To make Sauce: Heat sugar and water together until sugar dissolves. Add strawberries, simmer uncovered 5 minutes. Process in a food processor for 30 seconds or until smooth. Flavour with brandy or strawberry liqueur, to taste.

3 Heat oil in deep pan. Gently lower rounded tablespoons of batter into hot oil and cook over medium heat until fritters puff and turn golden brown. Drain on absorbent paper, dust with icing sugar.

4 Serve fritters with Strawberry Sauce and whipped cream.

Note: Use kiwi fruit mangoes, raspberries, passionfruit or blueberries instead of strawberries.

Stir flour into butter-sugar mixture in pan and beat until smooth.

Add strawberries to syrup and simmer uncovered for 5 minutes.

Gently lower rounded tablespoons of batter into hot oil.

Fritters will puff and turn golden brown. Drain on absorbent paper.

INDEX